Our
SAN FRANCISCO

Photography by Gary Crabbe
Text by Karen Misuraca

Voyageur Press

DEDICATIONS

To my darling Alyssa: I can't believe I got so lucky the second time around, so it seems only fitting to have my second book dedicated to you. And to my mother, Gloria, for everything you do and for always being there for my family. —GC

To Michael Capp, my partner in discovering the wonders of the world; and, to all of you who left your hearts in our beautiful San Francisco. —KM

Page 1: *Pierced by the Transamerica Pyramid, the city skyline is warmed at twilight by the terra cotta tones of the Palace of Fine Arts.*

Page 4: *Maple trees color a quiet footpath near Stowe Lake in Golden Gate Park, where San Franciscans enjoy a respite from city life.*

Page 5: *A fun way to ride about the city is on the colorful, historic streetcars. The city purchased restored, old streetcars from Milan, Italy, for popular tourist routes along the Embarcadero and up Market Street to the beach.*

Text © 2003 by Karen Misuraca
Photography © 2003 by Gary Crabbe

Edited by Amy Rost-Holtz
Designed by Maria Friedrich
Printed in China

03   04   05   06   07   5   4   3   2   1

Library of Congress Cataloging-in-Publication Data

Crabbe, Gary, 1964–
  Our San Francisco / photography by Gary Crabbe ; text by Karen Misuraca.
    p. cm.
  ISBN 0-89658-599-9 (hardcover)
  1. San Francisco (Calif.)—Pictorial works. 2. San Francisco (Calif.)—Description and travel. I. Misuraca, Karen. II. Title.
  F869.S343 C73 2003
  979.4'6—dc21
                                        2003000030

Distributed in Canada by Raincoast Books
9050 Shaughnessy Street, Vancouver, B.C. V6P 6E5

Published by Voyageur Press, Inc.
123 North Second Street, P.O. Box 338, Stillwater, MN 55082 U.S.A.
651-430-2210, fax 651-430-2211
books@voyageurpress.com
www.voyageurpress.com

Educators, fundraisers, premium and gift buyers, publicists, and marketing managers: Looking for creative products and new sales ideas? Voyageur Press books are available at special discounts when purchased in quantities, and special editions can be created to your specifications. For details contact the marketing department at 800-888-9653.

ACKNOWLEDGMENTS

$\mathcal{I}$ owe the greatest debt of thanks first to my wife, Connie, and to my mom, Gloria Crabbe, for they provided the greatest support and allowed me to take the time needed to photograph for this book. My thanks to Michelle Kingon and Phonh, whose helpful and trusted care of my son and daughter during the days while I was away made my work that much easier.

I'd also like to thank all the people who kindly allowed me to take their pictures as I wandered this magnificent city. To all of my "models," who were so gracious and understanding, you made shooting this book a wonderfully personal experience, even if our paths only crossed for a few brief minutes.

My thanks must go to Karen Misuraca, and to Amy Rost-Holtz and the wonderful people at Voyageur Press; it's been a true delight to work with you. I'd also like to give special thanks to Kimzey McGrath at the Marriott on Fourth Street, Julia Konstantinovsky at the Metreon, Tony Caparelli of the Great American Music Hall, Philip Allen of the Weinstein Gallery, Brian Frasier of Yerba Buena Arts & Events, and all the good people at the California Academy of Sciences, the American Conservatory Theater, The San Francisco Wax Museum, CityLight Books, and all the people who allowed my into their business, but did not make it into the book.

I'd also like to offer an extra thank you to Sean McCarty for all his great help, and to Barry Sundermeier for his friendship and companionship on my numerous excursions. I also want to offer a final note of thanks to Barbara and Galen; you helped me to see the light and find my path, and you will be greatly missed. —GC

Many thanks to our irrepressible, talented editor, Amy Rost-Holtz, and to Gary Crabbe for his high spirits, hard work, and timeless images. —KM

PHOTOGRAPHIC NOTES

$\mathcal{A}$ ll of the images created for this book were made with a 35mm SLR camera system. Specifically, I used either a Nikon 8008s or N90s camera body. I have a variety of lenses that range from a 24mm wide-angle lens to a 300mm telephoto lens, of which all are Nikon, save one Sigma 28–70 zoom lens. For images that required the use of a flash, I still use a trusty old Nikon SB-24 Speedlight, often connected to the camera using a SC-17 extension cord. In most cases my camera was attached to a Gitzo Carbon Fiber 1228 Mountaineer tripod, topped with a Slik Standard Ball Head II, and a Quick Release plate by Really Right Stuff. The only filters I use are a Circular Polarizer and a pair of Split Neutral Density Filters by Singh Ray. The ND filters are used to control the amount of light reaching part of the frame, without adding, altering, or changing the color, hence the term "neutral." All images have been recorded on professional transparency film, mostly Fuji RVP ASA 50, Fuji RFP 100, and Fuji RFP II. Film processing was done exclusively by The New Lab in San Francisco.

All images are accurate representations of the scenes before me when I took the photo, with the one exception being the shot of the full moon over the Golden Gate Bridge on page 16, which is an in-camera double exposure. —GC

CONTENTS

INTRODUCTION

My first memory of San Francisco is as a little girl, holding my mother's hand as we walked around Union Square in our best dresses, hats, and white gloves. We always started at the flower stand at Geary and Stockton, where Mom bought violets to pin to my coat and a gardenia for herself. We browsed the department stores—Macy's, I. Magnin, and the City of Paris—and stopped in at Shreve's, where the glittering jewelry showcases seemed like pirates' treasure chests to me.

At Christmastime, winter winds rustled the palms and yew trees, and we shivered in front of the spectacular window displays of skating bears whirling around mirrored ice rinks, live mannequins standing motionless in ball gowns, and choirs singing in snowy forest scenes. These were the "window wars," when the big stores spend thousands trying to outdo each other. They still do, every holiday season.

As a college student I discovered City Lights Booksellers in North Beach, where in the narrow aisles, long-haired Berkeley types read Allen Ginsberg, Jack Kerouac, and the Beat Generation poets. Today, City Lights

A fishing boat and the Maritime National Historical Park Museum gleam in the moonlight at Aquatic Park.

continues to sell and publish the best of what the alternative presses have to offer. San Francisco residents do, after all, buy more books per capita than in any other American city. Just across Columbus Avenue, Vesuvio's coffee house has been a fixture since 1949 and is still where the tragically wan, misunderstood intellectuals still congregate.

As young marrieds, my husband and I lingered beneath the lustrous, gold-leafed Gustave Klimt prints in the darkly romantic Redwood Room at the Clift Hotel. We went tea dancing at the Compass Rose among the potted palms at the St. Francis Hotel. Formerly a bastion of traditional elegance, the Clift was recently transformed into one of the hippest hotels on the West Coast. A minimalist, contempo–Art Deco invention, it has an Asian/Cuban restaurant and, in the bar, plasma-screen portraits with moving eyes and lips. The Compass Rose continues to hold forth in all its rococo, Renaissance Revival style, at the top of a sweeping, red-carpeted, marble staircase in the lobby of the circa 1904 St. Francis.

Years ago, we watched the flamboyant Seiji Ozawa conduct the San Francisco Symphony in the new Davies Symphony Hall, and we waltzed with the

FACING PAGE: *The symbol of San Francisco, the glowing, red-orange Golden Gate Bridge connects the city with the Marin Headlands.*

orchestra on the stage at "A Night in Old Vienna" on New Year's Eve. Since 1995, the charismatic Michael Tilson Thomas has led the symphony. Many consider MTT, as they call him here, the finest American conductor of his generation. Eclectic and adventurous, he has an affinity for Mahler, American and Russian repertory, and maverick composers, and a talent for attracting younger audiences to the concert hall.

The second-largest company in North America, the San Francisco Opera performs in a magnificent house that was completely refurbished in the late 1990s. The company has a history of debuts, including those of Birgit Nilsson, Leontyne Price, and Renata Tebaldi; conductor Georg Solti; and director Francis Ford Coppola.

During her college years, my middle daughter, Dia, lived in a basement apartment in the Haight-Ashbury District, a bohemian neighborhood of Victorian homes and tie-died T-shirt shops, made famous by the 1960s "Summer of Love." By the time she moved there, gentrification was underway and shops were being replaced by pricey boutiques and French-style bistros. No longer flophouses for runaways, some of the largest Victorians are now luxurious bed-and-breakfast inns. The most notable are the Archbishop's Mansion Inn—crowned by a sixteen-foot-tall stained-glass dome—and the Victorian Inn on the Park, a Queen Anne beauty built in 1897.

Speaking a cacophony of languages, residents of the Haight reflect the city's long-established diversity. San Francisco was founded by the Spanish; conquered by the Mexicans; and overrun by Europeans, South Americans, and Chinese in the forty-niner Gold Rush era. The city got in the habit of welcoming the immigrants who stream through its port, and airport, from all over the world. North Beach has the Italians, the Mission is Latino and Asian. On the west side in the "avenues" are the Russian immigrants, the Greeks, Armenians, Filipinos, Thais, Vietnamese, and Cambodians. Chinatown speaks for itself. Nowhere else in the United States will you find a wider variety of ethnic restaurants and markets—from Eritrean to Ethiopian and even Mesopotamian—and the only Tibetan restaurant west of the Rockies.

Multi-ethnic also, my grandchildren do not live in the City—everyone in San Francisco calls it "the City"—although they have, in a way, grown up here. Their favorite day is when we take the ferry from Larkspur on the north side of the bay, arrive at the Ferry Building at the foot of Market Street, and ride one of the vintage, Italian streetcars around the waterfront to Pier 39 to watch the street performers and the sea lions at K Dock.

From the waterfront, we ride a cable car up and over Telegraph Hill, past Union Square, and walk the few blocks to Yerba Buena Gardens. Above the lawns and trees and

Residents of Chinatown enjoy the cherry blossoms in April.

outdoor sculpture, on a magical terrace that seems to float among the skyscrapers surrounding it, is one of the most impressive commitments to young people ever made by an American city—the Rooftop, which comprises an ice arena, a bowling center, and a space-age playground. Leonardo da Vinci meets R2-D2 at Zeum, the pumpkin-and-mauve-colored visual, performing, and media arts center for teens, while gilded creatures twirl in a glass box on a 1906 Charles Looff carousel.

When we can't play another minute, we either lie on the greensward or take in an IMAX movie here at Sony's Metreon. This mega-entertainment center contains restaurants, shops, and a children's world of interactive play, from high-tech gadgets at the Sony Style store to Maurice Sendak's "Where the Wild Things Are" to surreal, electronic games and karaoke for your feet at Dance Dance Revolution.

My granddaughters sip tea from tiny cups in the Japanese Tea Garden in Golden Gate Park under pink clouds of cherry blossoms, just as I did at their ages. While I, as a child, wandered the halls of the de Young Museum past the dark Rembrandts, these kids tromp around the Mexican Museum, which vibrates with the bright colors of masks, outrageous papier-mâché animals, and Day-of-the-Dead figures. A new home for the museum will soon be a red-orange, cubed complex designed by Mexico City architect, Ricardo Legorreta.

These little girls wouldn't be caught dead wearing white gloves—a baseball glove at Pacific Bell Park, maybe. They like "walkaway" crab cocktails at Fisherman's Wharf, walking across the Golden Gate Bridge, and quirky stuff, like the Wave Organ. A strange instrument played by the tides of the bay, it is constructed of a jumble of Victorian tombstones and plastic pipes through which the sea waters rush in and out, creating echoing, gurgling sounds, as if from the bowels of the earth. The Wax Museum is also high on their sightseeing list. A spooky, touristy, movielike setting, the museum is home to nearly three hundred celebrities and historical figures in the (waxed) flesh, including Princess Diana, Cinderella, Elvis, Michael Jackson, Marilyn Monroe, and Joe DiMaggio.

My grandson goes for the albino crocodile at the Academy of Sciences. He also likes the swords, guns, and cannons at the Civil War–era Fort Point, built under the Golden Gate Bridge to protect the city from a sea attack that never came. Fort Point is a good place to get photos of the bridge, with waves crashing in the foreground and windsurfers in the bay. You can also fish here along the seawall.

We follow tourists into the mysterious nooks and crannies of Chinatown. We stand in line to eat tacos at La Taqueria in the Mission, sit up at the counter for Dungeness crab at Swan's Oyster Depot, and sip thick malteds at St. Francis Fountain.

Fourth of July at the waterfront on the Marina Green is a tradition. The sky is filled with vividly colored, Asian-style kites. The bay flutters with sailboarders and flags on hundreds of sailboats, motor yachts, ferries, and often an aircraft carrier. The fireworks seem always to disappear into the July fog. As Mark Twain said, "The coldest winter I ever spent was one summer in San Francisco."

September and October are the best months, when days are sparkling clear and warm and a flock of outdoor events take place: a food-and-wine tasting extravaganza in Golden Gate Park, called A La Carte A La Park; the San Francisco Blues Festival at Fort Mason; a Latino festival in the Mission; and the Festival of the Sea on the Hyde Street Pier. The fine weather holds for the Columbus Day parade, for two weeks of live performances at the San Francisco Jazz Festival, and for Fleet Week, when the Blue Angels and vintage aircraft dazzle crowds with air shows over the bay.

As Frank Sinatra said of San Francisco, "Now there's a grown-up, swinging town!"

Everyone has a great view of the fireworks from their brilliant, hillside amphitheater of bay windows.

ABOVE: *Unique for its time, the flatiron-style Columbus Tower, built in 1905, is a charming contrast to the 853-foot-tall Transamerica Pyramid. Erected in 1972 amid great controversy due its striking silhouette, the forty-eight-story pyramid is clad in eight stories of gleaming white quartz, narrowing to a 212-foot aluminum spire.*

RIGHT: *Just west of the Golden Gate Bridge, the Sea Cliff residential district was laid out in 1912 to take advantage of panoramic bay views.*

FACING PAGE: *A glance at a map shows that San Francisco is married to the Pacific Ocean. The long, sandy stretch of Ocean Beach bravely faces the Pacific, while a forest of piers and wharves reach out into San Francisco Bay.*

ABOVE: *Pleasure boaters bounce over the choppy waters of San Francisco Bay near the island of Alcatraz, where tourists visit the former federal prison and enjoy stunning views of the Bay Area.*

LEFT: *From the Gold Rush until the 1930s when the bridges were built, as many as fifty ferries crisscrossed San Francisco Bay. Today, commuters enjoy relaxing cruises to and from work, while tourists "baytrip" under the bridges to Alcatraz and Angel Island, Marin County, and the East Bay.*

A Colorful Past: History and Landmarks

The largest protected bay for a thousand miles, San Francisco Bay determined this city's fate. Spanish explorers sailed through the Golden Gate by accident in 1769 to find a vast, sheltered body of water fed by the mighty Sacramento River. They built a garrison—the Presidio—and Mission Dolores, and they settled in.

Mexico took over in 1821, holding sway until 1846, when American sailors from the warship *Portsmouth* ran the Stars and Stripes up the Presidio flagpole. American pioneers and gold seekers from around the world came and stayed. The harbor began to fill with wooden ships and the hills with tents and hardscrabble shacks. The tin-pot settlement turned into a boomtown overnight.

Silver barons built mansions and hotels, and financed the transcontinental railroad, opening the city to a gilded age of expansion, with skyscrapers sprouting up and ferries crisscrossing the bay. Nearly destroyed by the earthquake of 1906, the city rose like a phoenix, welcoming the world to the 1915 International Exposition. A spectacular Beaux-Arts–style Civic Center and two bay-spanning bridges rose in the 1930s.

Today, the city's seagoing, fortune-hunting, earthquaking history is preserved in its world-famous landmarks and monuments.

A sweep of cable, iron, and steel, the Golden Gate Bridge represents the open arms of a city that has welcomed immigrants, fortune seekers, and admirers for over a century and a half.

FACING PAGE: *Climbing up from the waterfront, cable cars are good platforms from which to view the city's world-famous bridges and islands.*

ABOVE: *"I don't know who decided to paint it orange, but God bless them. When you drive up over 19th Avenue and see the bridge rising before you, it's like seeing the towers of Chartres when you're driving out of Paris."* —*Susan Cheever,* Home Before Dark

RIGHT: *San Francisco is famous for romantic fogs. When the fog is thick and the seas are gray, they seem to flow together and silently cover the city, with only the lighted towers of the Golden Gate Bridge peeking out over the moist swells. Summer mornings and evenings are often chilly, when misty fingers creep in through the mile-wide Golden Gate, the city's natural air-conditioner.*

At the Civil War–era Fort Point National Historic Site under the Golden Gate Bridge, costumed docents and park rangers give tours of the gunpowder storehouse, barracks, jail cells, and a museum of military artifacts. For decades the fort housed sentries and soldiers, alert for a sea attack that never came.

ALL PHOTOS: *Built during the Gold Rush of the mid 1800s, thousands of gabled, turreted, gingerbread-trimmed Victorian mansions are the "Painted Ladies" of San Francisco. Grand old houses on Nob Hill and in the Alamo Square and Pacific Heights neighborhoods are painted and prettied up, from their fretwork cornices to their filigreed verandahs, friezes, and stained glass windows.*

Hop aboard a cable car, the nation's only mobile National Historic Landmark, for a slow cruise from Union Square over Nob Hill and down to the waterfront. The clanging bell and the screeching grip-and-release brakes are part of fun as you whip around an S-curve at a sizzling nine miles per hour.

Since 1873, when cable cars first trundled up and down the steep hills of the city, visitors have wondered how the more than three dozen cars are pulled over miles of track. The mystery is solved at the Cable Car Barn and Museum, a bright red, brick barn where huge wheels drive the winding machinery, reeling eleven miles of steel at a steady pace of nine and a half miles per hour.

ABOVE: *A WPA project built during the Depression, 210-foot-tall, Art Deco–style Coit Tower is adorned inside with vivid murals of laborers in early California. Visitors get views of the north Bay Area, the Golden Gate, the Bay Bridge, and Alcatraz from the top of a tower.*

LEFT: *The bronze statue of Christopher Columbus was a gift to the city from the local Italian community.*

ABOVE: *Said to be the greatest collection of French High Baroque Revival architecture in the country, the impressive Civic Center buildings are splendidly floodlit at night. Completed in 1915 in the architectural boom that followed the great earthquake of 1906, the City Hall sports a golden dome, sweeping marble staircases, filigreed iron and gilt banisters, and an elaborately decorated, four-story rotunda.*

RIGHT: *Among the most flamboyant of landmarks, the Palace of Fine Arts is a remnant of the 1915 Panama Pacific International Exposition, when a newly rebuilt San Francisco welcomed the world just nine years after the earthquake that destroyed much of the city. Standing today in a small park in the Marina District, the palace is a classical Roman temple with two colonnades, reflected in a small lake swimming with swans.*

ABOVE AND RIGHT: *Originally occupied by Spanish and Mexican armies, the Presidio was the treasured preserve of the U.S. Army until 1994 when it became part of the National Park Service. Rangers lead tours of the grounds, museums, and architectural relics, from seventeenth-century bronze Spanish cannons to Civil War barracks, pre-earthquake Victorians, and picturesque rows of Queen Anne–style officer's homes.*

ABOVE: *On a hillside framed by Monterey cypress, the San Francisco National Cemetery in the Presidio is the resting place of military heroes and foot soldiers from early Western frontier camps, the Spanish-American War, the Civil War, two World Wars, and other conflicts.*

ALL PHOTOS: *Isolated by the treacherous waters of San Francisco Bay, Alcatraz was a federal maximum-security prison nicknamed "The Rock" and housing such notorious gangsters as Al Capone, George "Machine Gun" Kelly, the "Birdman of Alcatraz," and hundreds of others. Now part of the Golden Gate National Recreation Area, Alcatraz draws more than a million visitors a year to prowl the dank stone and concrete cells and look through iron bars at a prisoner's tantalizing view of the city and freedom. Park rangers, and, sometimes, former guards and prisoners are on hand to lead tours.*

FACING PAGE: *Fisherman's Wharf once bustled with Sicilian and Genoese fishermen unloading their catches to sell off the boats. Today you can catch a glimpse and a sniff of the fishing fleet and taste seafood in the nearby restaurants and markets. The catches are primarily squid, sole, sea bass, cod, and halibut, with salmon, shrimp, and the fabled Dungeness crab caught seasonally.*

ABOVE: *Go down to Fisherman's Wharf to a crab stand and pick out a big, pink Dungeness crab. The "cracker" will cook it in his pot, clean it, and tap each shell segment lightly with his mallet. He will give you a lemon, and you can eat the crab right there in sight of the fishing fleet.*

LEFT: *Tourists flock to Fisherman's Wharf for seafood restaurants, souvenir stores, museums, salty air, shopping malls, and such attractions as the Wax Museum and Ripley's Believe It or Not.*

At Pier 39 are more than a hundred shops and restaurants, from Field of Dreams sports collectibles to rock-and-roll memorabilia at The Beat Goes On, and Bubba Gump Shrimp Company.

Handcrafted in Italy, elegant gondolas and rocking ponies glide around the double-decker, Venetian carousel at Pier 39.

BOTH PHOTOS: *A ferry returns from a tour of San Francisco Bay while sea lions lounge on "K Dock" at the end of Pier 39. Protected by the Federal Marine Protection Act, the sea lion population grows as high as 900 during the winter.*

FACING PAGE: *Opened in 1936, the Oakland Bay Bridge received a sparkling necklace of 860 globes on its graceful suspension cables in honor of its fiftieth birthday. Anchored by financial district high-rises, the eastern waterfront blazes with light as the sun sets.*

TOP LEFT: *A family enjoys the beach at Aquatic Park. In the background is the Hyde Street Pier, America's only floating national park. Knot-tying, sail-raising, and sea chantey singing take place on the 1886 square-rigger,* Balclutha.

BOTTOM LEFT: *Looking for all the world like a cruise ship about to set sail into the bay, the Streamline Moderne–style Maritime National Historical Park Museum was built by the WPA in the 1930s. Its exhibits feature ship models, figureheads, maritime paintings, photos, and relics such as scrimshaw and ships in bottles.*

In the Neighborhoods: People and Places

Walking is the best way to explore this city of ethnic neighborhoods and historic districts. From the *taquerias* in the Mission District to the *trattorias* in North Beach, the mysterious temples in Chinatown, the noodle shops in the "avenues," the sushi bars in Japantown, and the rainbow flags of the Castro, San Francisco is joyously cosmopolitan.

Clinging to steep streets on Telegraph Hill are vintage apartment buildings and little wooden houses—once fishermen's shacks—snug with cottage gardens. Once a grubby industrial port area, South Beach is now a stylish stretch of condominiums, brew pubs, cafes, and shops—a trendy new neighborhood. Old money built Pacific Heights, a bastion of Victorian mansions with lacy trim, turrets, and gables. Whimsical Art Nouveau facades line up on Nob Hill, sometimes called "Snob Hill."

"People from around the world have adopted San Francisco as their home and brought with them the tastes, styles, and traditions of their heritage," says Jeff Clarke, president of KQED Public Broadcasting. "The resulting composition is a fascinating experiment in twenty-first-century cultural diversity."

Building-sized murals are part of the lively arts scene of the multi-ethnic Mission District.

FACING PAGE: *In a sprawling grid running up hills and down valleys, city streets are steep, often ending on wooded hilltops and sometimes in stairs that residents trudge up to their apartment buildings and their great views.*

A pale moon hangs over apartment buildings on Telegraph and Russian Hills. The city is apartment-oriented, with about 65 percent of all San Francisco housing renter-occupied.

Cars and tourists amble down the crookedest street in town, brick-paved Lombard Street on Telegraph Hill.

On the Pacific side of the city from the tip of Fort Funston, the view is of Ocean Beach and the Sunset District. When locals speak of "the avenues," they mean the streets in the flat Sunset and Richmond residential districts, which are numerically named, like Sixth and Seventh Avenues.

A high, modern pagoda towers above a miniature Ginza known as Nihonmachi or Japantown, three square blocks of shops, restaurants, galleries, movie theaters, Japanese baths, and the Miyako Hotel.

The blood-racing percussion beat and striking poses of the Taiko drummers create drama at the annual Nihonmachi Street Fair in Japantown.

Bonsai trees are on sale and display at the street fair.

Top right: *Vintage movies are on the marquee at the Castro Theater, where the audience gets into the act by repeating favorite lines of dialogue, hooting, and cat-calling, all in fun.*

Bottom right: *The entire neighborhood comes out to the Castro Street Fair for swing dancing, Latin rhythms, and country western bands at the non-stop dancing pavilions. Funds raised by food and beverage vendors and at the kissing booth are donated to local charities.*

Facing page: *In the Castro District, the gay community holds forth in rainbow colors and a cacophony of bars and restaurants, bookstores and boutiques housed in refurbished Victorians.*

Fruits, flowers, and vegetables thrive right in the middle of the crowded city as part of a community garden in the Marina District.

San Francisco Bay is a great place to wet your rail, say the yacht and sailboat owners at the small-craft harbor in the Marina District.

Stroll around the Marina District to see Mediterranean Revival, Moderne, and Art Deco homes and apartment buildings from the 1920s and 1930s.

Mission Dolores Park is a precious patch of greensward in the highly congested, multi-ethnic Mission District.

Wildly colorful, sometimes political, always whimsical, slashes of Latin American life appear on more than two hundred buildings, fences and walls in the Mission District. Definitely not graffiti, this is one of the most exciting and important art collections in the West.

Saint Francis of Assisi is patron saint of Mission Dolores and San Francisco. In a lovely little garden cemetery at the mission lie thousands of the Mexican, Spanish, Indian, and Irish builders of the early city.

The Italian population of North Beach assembles on Columbus Avenue to discuss issues of the day.

The ghosts of Allen Ginsberg, Jack Kerouac, and the Beat Generation poets of the 1950s haunt the crowded aisles and book-lined rooms of City Lights, a legendary bookstore. A stellar figure from the heyday of the North Beach literati, owner Lawrence Ferlinghetti holds forth in his labyrinth of book-lined rooms, where poetry readings and author events are standing room only.

ABOVE, RIGHT: *In Molinari's Delicatessen in North Beach, the aromas of dozens of varieties of Italian cheeses and salamis are as intoxicating as a glass of Chianti.*

TOP LEFT AND ABOVE: *The rich smells of Graffeo coffee, meatball sandwiches, and home-made focaccia waft down Columbus Avenue in North Beach. Once the bailiwick of Italian fisherman, the avenue is now a warren of family-style Italian ristorantes, pizza joints, bakeries, and coffee houses. In some, the staff sings opera. In others, you hear the click of pinball and pool. Survivors from the 1950s bohemian days are Spec's 12 Adler Museum Cafe and Mario's Bohemian Cigar Store.*

ABOVE: *The blood red, bright yellow, and green neon signs; pagoda roofs; and dragon-bedecked lampposts of Chinatown signify health, wealth, and good luck. Flying from the rooftops are banners and flags heralding the family associations—the* hui-kuan—*that unite Chinese with a common heritage.*

RIGHT: *An elaborate movie theater in the 1940s, the SunSing Center on Grant Avenue is now crowded with vendors selling flowers and souvenirs.*

ABOVE: *The annual Chinese New Year Parade in February is glowing lanterns, crashing cymbals, marching bands, booming drum troupes, and the famous dragons.*

LEFT: *Ferocious carved dogs guard the Chinatown Gate, which leads to one of the city's oldest streets, Grant Avenue. Larger souvenir stores and antique emporiums are on Grant, while fragrant herb shops and trading companies hide in a labyrinth of forty-one narrow alleys.*

BOTH PHOTOS: *The home of the Grateful Dead and the Jefferson Airplane in the 1960s, the Haight-Ashbury District was inhabited by long-haired peaceniks wearing tie-dyed shirts, antiwar buttons, and flowers in their hair. Vestiges of the counterculture remain in coffeehouses and psychedelic crystal shops, while the rows of Victorian houses are remodeled for a new generation.*

BOTH PHOTOS: *In today's Haight-Ashbury, secondhand clothing stores are now classy vintage apparel shops. Trendy bistros have replaced cheap cafes. On weekends, artisans set up shop on the sidewalks, and multi-ethnic, middle-class couples walk their babies and dogs.*

ABOVE: *Built atop Nob Hill of Connecticut brownstone, which saved it from the 1906 fire, the 1886 neoclassical James Flood mansion is now a private men's club guarded by an elaborate bronze fence.*

RIGHT: *In Huntington Park on Nob Hill, bronze turtles, dolphins, and ephebes play on a replica of the curvaceous Tartarughe Fountain in Rome.*

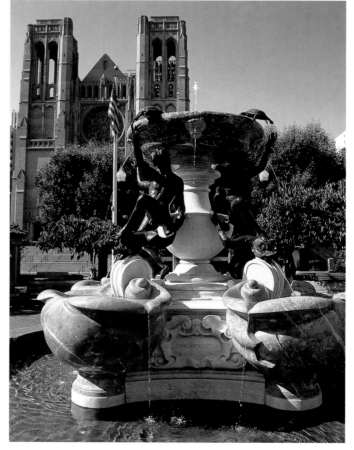

LEFT: *Medieval-style, stained-glass windows create glorious multi-colored light in the vast nave of the Neo-Gothic Grace Cathedral on Nob Hill. The magnificent rose window, called "Canticle to the Sun," was created by Gabriel Loire of Chartres, France. Exact replicas of the famous fifteenth-century doors of the Baptistry in Florence, Italy, the bronze "Doors of Paradise" depict scenes from the Old Testament.*

BELOW: *A Beaux-Arts beauty, the Fairmont Hotel holds forth in grand style, as it has since 1907. In the cavernous lobby are sweeping staircases, soaring ceilings, marble columns, and a valuable art collection.*

The Urban Landscape: Business and Architecture

Sliding toward the Pacific, the setting sun illuminates a skyline of many eras, reflecting the spirit of a city that has since its birth risked everything for the main chance. In the financial and cultural capital of the West, the architecture is meant to impress.

Palatial mansions were built for the silver kings of the 1800s. The tallest building west of the Mississippi in 1898, the Ferry Building remains today headquarters for the Port of San Francisco. A golden-domed, neo-classical City Hall and the templelike Pacific Coast Stock Exchange rose in 1915. Fancy with tiles and terra-cotta in Art Deco and Spanish Mediterranean themes, apartment buildings from the 1920s and 1930s line the streets of toney neighborhoods. Skyscrapers grew on the eastern waterfront in the twentieth century. The silvery Transamerica Pyramid shines against the dark glass facade of the Bank of America's former headquarters.

Visitors overlook the city from the View Lounge at the top of the San Francisco Marriott Hotel, a popular businessperson's hostelry near the Moscone Convention Center.

More than the sum of her history and architectural landmarks, San Francisco stands on her hills above the bay with high expectations. As Edward Mace wrote in the *Observer,* "You get the impression that if the place were chosen as the setting for the Second Coming, the citizens would be pleased but not surprised."

FACING PAGE: *Sunset paints the sky as traffic builds on Columbus Avenue at Broadway, a confluence of the bohemian neighborhood of North Beach and the Financial District.*

The Financial District dominates the eastern bayfront. The commercial and cultural center of the greater Bay Area, San Francisco is also financial headquarters for new California gold, the high-tech Silicon Valley—the birthplace of the personal computer—a few miles to the south.

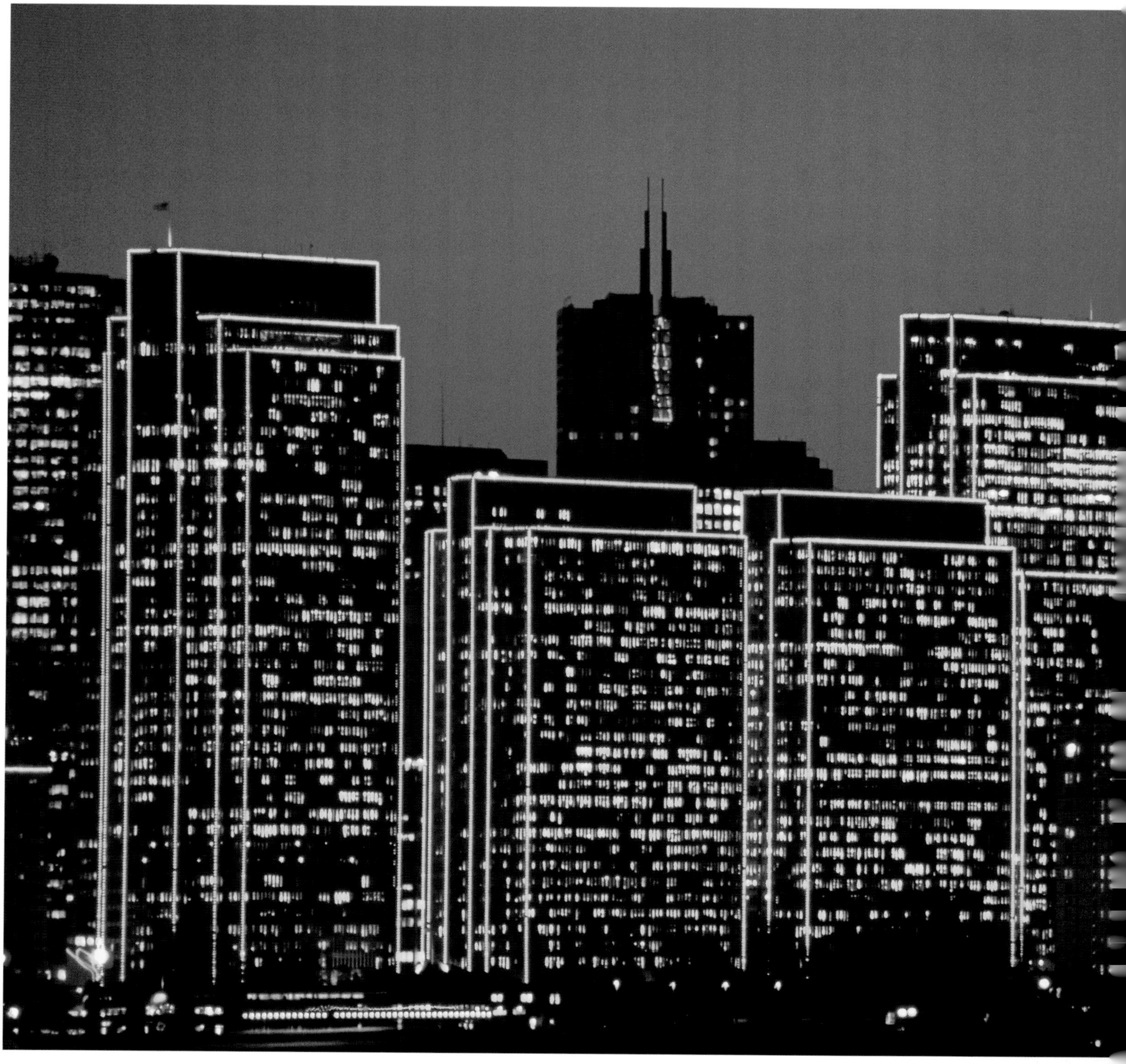

ABOVE: *Travelers flying into San Francisco after dark look down on a glittering eastern skyline when the glass monoliths of Embarcadero Center, the Transamerica Pyramid, and Financial District high-rises are ablaze from top to bottom.*

LEFT: *On crisp, clear December nights, Christmas shoppers converge on Macy's at Union Square.*

Once solely warehouses, factories, and rundown hotels, the South of Market Area (SOMA) was dramatically revitalized. Luxury high-rise hotels and office towers, major museums, new theaters and shopping complexes have turned urban blight into a glittering new city-within-a-city.

Modeled after Milan's Galleria Vittorio Emanuele, the airy and ornate Crocker Galleria downtown comprises boutiques from Versace to Ralph Lauren. The city's number one industry, tourism, supports a multitude of high-end shops, art galleries, department stores and shopping centers on the streets around Union Square.

Distinctive post-Moderne-style fan windows top the granite and glass monolith of the San Francisco Marriott Hotel at Yerba Buena Gardens.

Gleaming white against skyscrapers twice its size, Willis Polk's elegant 1914 design for the Hobart Building on Market Street was shaped for a polygonal site.

Where Chinatown and the Financial District meet, the Transamerica Pyramid is a slender foil to pagoda-like towers and the Gothic Revival–style Old St. Mary's Church.

Erected on Market Street in 1897, and surviving the 1906 earthquake to strike a silhouette against twentieth-century high-rises, the Native Sons Monument honors California's admission into the Union in 1850.

Walkers, runners, cyclists, and baby strollers share the salty air and the sea breezes along the palm-fringed Embarcadero, one of the grandest waterfront promenades in the world. Office workers inhabit the upper floors of Embarcadero Center, dazzling interconnected high-rise towers. Within the center are hundreds of shops and restaurants; public rooftop gardens; and an array of outdoor art.

Modeled after the Giralda Tower in Seville, Spain, the 235-foot-high clock tower of the Ferry Building is a symbol of the Port of San Francisco, a major trade gateway to Mexico, Latin America, and the Pacific Rim. Fireboat crews miraculously saved the tower from the 1906 fire; old photos show the spear-shaped building wreathed in smoke at the end of a ruined Market Street.

LEFT: *Steam-powered paddlewheelers tie up at the waterfront and take passengers around the bay. When the boats were built before the turn of the nineteenth century, customs houses, gambling establishments, and businesses were built on landfill created in the bay by the skeletons of abandoned sailing ships.*

ABOVE: *Financial District high-rises loom above a lonely pier at sunset on the Embarcadero.*

Built in 1914, St. Ignatius Church at the University of San Francisco is an Italian Renaissance–style cathedral.

ABOVE: *Four 190-foot-tall hyperbolic paraboloids top St. Mary's Cathedral on Geary Boulevard.*

LEFT: *The gold-leafed onion domes of the Russian Holy Virgin Cathedral of the Church in Exile is the largest Russian Orthodox church on the Pacific Coast.*

THE LIVELY ARTS: MUSIC, DRAMA, MUSEUMS

Anchored by a quartet of powerhouse museums—the Museum of Modern Art, the Asian Museum, the M. H. deYoung Museum, and the Palace of the Legion of Honor—San Francisco's life in art is rich in both tradition and innovation. Bedrock sources of money from the city's founding families, today's high-income baby boomers, and a steady flow of sophisticated international visitors support the museums and hundreds of art galleries.

The gallery scene is brilliantly reflective of a history of experimentation and multi-culturalism. First defined by the "Revolution and Evolution" culture of the 1960s that remains alive and kicking today, it is continually redefined by the high-tech and new media bent of young artists from Bay Area art schools, and by the influx of talented Asian and Hispanic immigrants.

World-class opera, symphony, and ballet companies, and one of the leading regional theaters in the country, lead the myriad of internationally known theater, dance, and musical institutions. Beyond the classics, the city's ethnic diversity and tolerance of alternative lifestyles create an arts community of futurists and upstarts.

Bronze lions guard the Palace of the Legion of Honor, which shelters 4,000 years of ancient and European art.

FACING PAGE: *The glitterati assemble in their evening gowns and tuxedos on opening night at the opera, the highlight of the fall social season.*

ABOVE: *An ornate, Baroque Revival jewel modeled after the Paris Opera and built in 1932, the War Memorial Opera House provided a grand setting for the signing of the United Nations Charter in 1945.*

RIGHT: *A production of the American Conservatory Theater (A.C.T.), "A Christmas Carol" is a holiday tradition. Over thirty-five years of Tony Award–winning productions make A.C.T. one of the premier regional theater companies in the country. Mainstream dramas and musical comedies are performed in the elegant Edwardian-style Geary Theater.*

A museum-caliber collection of twentieth-century masters, such as Picasso, Chagall, Matta, and Miro, make the Weinstein Gallery near Union Square an exciting place to discover art. The city's gallery scene reflects a history of experimentation and multi-culturalism.

BOTH PHOTOS: *Built in 1924 as a memorial to World War I dead, the Palace of the Legion of Honor stands in a spectacular wooded setting with panoramic views of the Golden Gate. The building is styled after the eighteenth-century Palais de Legion d'Honneur in Paris.*

A dazzling Modernist temple to the arts, the San Francisco Museum of Modern Art was designed by Swiss architect Mario Botta. An upslanting cylinder soars from the roof, allowing light to pour into the atrium and throughout a whirl of galleries. The museum showcases the works of Matisse, Picasso, Warhol, and other modern masters.

ABOVE: *A whirl of vivid colors and gilt in a glass pavilion, the 1903 Charles Looff carousel at Yerba Buena Gardens spins like a kaleidoscope.*

LEFT: *Art larger than life, Maurice Sendak's friendly, scary creatures inhabit "Where the Wild Things Are" in Sony's Metreon entertainment complex. Younger children crawl through a maze, peek into a bubbling cauldron, and talk to a seventeen-foot-high puppet.*

ABOVE: *Bette Davis, Lucille Ball, and nearly three hundred more celebrities and historical figures look you right in the eye at the Wax Museum on Fisherman's Wharf.*

RIGHT: *A bordello in the Roaring Twenties, a nightclub where stripper Sally Rand took it all off in the 1930s, the gilded, ornate Great American Music Hall is a popular downtown venue for concerts, comedy nights, and dance parties.*

The longest continuously running blues festival in the country, the San Francisco Blues Festival takes place on the Great Meadow at Fort Mason, with spectacular views of the bay and the Golden Gate Bridge, passing ships and sailboats.

During the Fillmore's hard-rock heyday in the 1960s and 1970s, the late rock promoter Bill Graham collected psyche-delic-style posters of the Jefferson Airplane, the Beatles, and the Grateful Dead. Today's hall presents such bands as Jefferson Starship, Los Lobos, and local stars Boz Scaggs, Santana, and Metallica.

PLAYING AROUND: PARKS, GARDENS, AND THE OUTDOORS

In this compact city of hills, open spaces are prized and well used, from a block-square patch of neighborhood park to the stretch of Ocean Beach on the Pacific side of the city. In all, San Francisco has nearly two hundred public parks. The crowning glory of it all, Golden Gate Park is one of the world's largest and most beautiful urban preserves. Stretching nearly four miles to the sea in a wide swath of meadows, hills, forests, flower gardens, and lakes, it is a precious retreat from concrete and city life.

A breezy footpath, the Coastal Trail traces the rugged cliffs at the entrance to San Francisco Bay. Entirely paved, the Golden Gate Promenade winds along the bayfront from Fort Point to Aquatic Park. Bikers and skaters cruise around Lake Merced. Walking is the best way to see and enjoy the more than 350 wooden, stone, and concrete stairways that connect steep streets on the city's forty-two hills; bordering the stairways is a hidden world of trees, residential gardens, and the few wild areas.

Ghirardelli Square is a shopping and restaurant complex on the waterfront that has won design awards for the appealing way it wraps around two central garden plazas.

FACING PAGE: *The Camera Obscura at Ocean Beach is an unusual, Leonardo da Vinci–designed invention that you step into to watch the sea life offshore.*

ABOVE: *Built for the 1894 California Mid-winter International Exposition, the Spreckles Temple of Music in Golden Gate Park is the site of free outdoor concerts, festivals, and dance performances.*

FACING PAGE: *Built in 1895, the Japanese Tea Garden in Golden Gate Park is the oldest public Japanese-style garden in America. Visitors can wander amid a fantasy of cherry trees, dark pines, lily ponds swimming with carp, a graceful Moon Bridge, and a brightly painted and gilded, five-level pagoda. In spring, cherry blossoms are a fragrant cloud, and the rhododendrons and azaleas are oceans of magenta, pink, and white.*

Ferocious life-size dinosaurs, giant insects, and prehistoric humans come to life at the California Academy of Sciences in Golden Gate Park.

Tropical foliage and a waterfall create a natural, watery environment for crocodiles, poison dart frogs, Burmese pythons, and snapping turtles at the Steinhart Aquarium in Golden Gate Park.

LEFT: *You can rent a small boat and cruise around picturesque Stowe Lake, then stop on Strawberry Hill.*

ABOVE: *In 1871, a vast, sandy plot on the west side of the city was transformed into Golden Gate Park by an inspired engineer, William Hall, and a heroic master gardener, John McLaren. They created forests, glades, and meandering roads and footpaths, planting tens of thousands of trees and shrubs, and more than six thousand flower species from around the world. Flower lovers head for the specialty gardens, including the Strybing Arboretum and the Conservatory of Flowers in a monumental Victorian glass house.*

Brought from the Netherlands in the late 1800s, windmills once pumped water to irrigate Golden Gate Park. Now they create a picturesque backdrop for seasonal flower displays.

California gulls accompany the slow, graceful practice of tai chi at Spreckels Lake in Golden Gate Park.

ABOVE: *No other baseball stadium in the world has the setting of Pacific Bell Park, with vistas of San Francisco Bay, the Oakland Bay Bridge, and the city skyline. Some right field, home-run balls actually end up with the fishes in McCovey Cove. Outside the park, fans line up at portholes to watch games at no charge. In the city's tradition of serving the best food on the planet, vendors in the stadium sell everything from cappuccinos to gourmet burritos, cheesecake, and chili.*

Left: *Intrepid San Francisco 49er football fans bundle up against the freezing winds at 3Com Park on the bay, south of the city.*

Reflecting the city's upbeat and diverse character, runners and walkers throng through the streets in the annual Bay to Breakers, the world's largest, and possibly the most bizarre, footrace.

At the foot of the Ferry Building, Justin Herman Plaza is transformed into Kristi Yamaguchi Embarcadero Center Ice Rink during the holidays. Yamaguchi and her Olympic-medal-winning friends skate with the locals.

ABOVE: *At the San Francisco Zoo, the world's largest naturalistic gorilla exhibit shelters a family of lowland gorillas, including an adult male silverback and adorable youngsters. The zoo exhibits rare and endangered animals such as black rhinos, snow leopards, condors, and casqued hornbills.*

RIGHT: *Penguins line up for a fishy lunch at the San Francisco Zoo.*

One of the pop icons of the city, the two-hundred-pound, fiberglass Doggie Diner head is one of two remaining from a chain of 1960s hot dog stands.

Lincoln Park Golf Course opened in 1910 when residents were turning in their horse-drawn carriages for Model Ts. Fairways twist between tall eucalyptus and pines, riding the hilly terrain like rodeo broncos.

A four-mile walking and biking road circles Lake Merced, a freshwater reservoir near Ocean Beach. You can launch your own small nonmotorized vessel, or rent a rowboat and fish for catfish, trout, and bass.

Serving up seafood and spectacular sea views, the Cliff House perches on the western edge of the city at Ocean Beach.

The sun sinks into the Pacific while cormorants gather on the offshore rocks near Ocean Beach.

In the 1880s, sun-warmed glass enclosed huge, seawater swimming pools at Sutro Baths at Land's End. Only ruins remain there now, but a gallery of antique photos at the nearby Cliff House Restaurant show the baths in their heyday.

A four-mile-long ribbon of sand along the western edge of the city, Ocean Beach is popular for walking, running, and sunbathing—or fogbathing. The water is extremely cold and the undertow is treacherous. Swimming is prohibited, although you may see an occasional foolhardy surfer. Besides sea gulls, inhabitants include the Western Snowy Plover, a threatened species of shorebird.

A breezy park on the bayfront, Crissy Field is a place to walk and in-line skate, sit on a narrow beach, and watch the boats and the windsurfers.

Thousands of trees were planted in the Presidio a century ago, making this precious piece of open space a haven for bikers and hikers.

Above the Pacific Ocean at the western edge of the city, the Coastal Trail is a nine-mile footpath from the Golden Gate Bridge to Fort Funston.

Baker Beach stretches a mile along the western shore of the Presidio. Views of the Golden Gate and the Marin Headlands are stunning, and the fishing is good for surf perch and striped bass. Hot days are rare, and pounding surf make ocean swimming inadvisable around the city, except at tiny China Beach and in the protected cove of Aquatic Park.

About the Photographer and Author

Gary Crabbe has been taking pictures of majestic landscapes and travel destinations in the western United States for the last ten years. Based in the San Francisco Bay Area, he is the owner of Enlightened Images Photography and is the photographer of Voyageur Press's *The California Coast* (2001). His publication credits and clients include the National Geographic Society, the *New York Times*, Forbes, the North Face, L.L. Bean, *Sunset Magazine*, the Nature Conservancy, and the Carnegie Museum of Natural History. He sells his work as fine art prints, wall murals, stock, and assignment photography traditionally and through his website, www.enlightphoto.com.

Karen Misuraca is a travel, golf, and outdoor writer based in Sonoma, in the heart of California's Wine Country. When not exploring the streets of San Francisco, she contributes articles to a variety of publications, including *Alaska Airlines Magazine*, *Horizon Air*, TravelClassics.com, *Distinction*, and others. She is the author of *The 100 Best Golf Resorts of the World*, *CitySmart San Francisco*, *Quick Escapes from San Francisco*, *Insiders' Guide to Yosemite*, *Fun With the Family in Northern California*, and *The California Coast* (Voyageur Press, 2001). She is accompanied on her forays into San Francisco by her three daughters, a lively contingent of grandchildren, and her partner, Michael Capp.